The Bird Chart Boy

Also by James J. Raciti

Poetry:

Charles
Dabs of Myself

Fiction:

Au Revoir à la France
Giacomo
Legacy of War
Pulling No Ponchos

Non-fiction:

Old Santa Fe
Ask About Santa Fe
Ask About Florida
Carrabelle and Florida's Forgotten Coast

Plays:

Invitation to Dawn
The Song of Roland

The Bird Chart Boy

New and Selected Poems

James J. Raciti

SUNSTONE
PRESS

SANTA FE

Sunstone books may be purchased for educational, business, or sales promotional use.
For information please write: Special Markets Department, Sunstone Press,
P.O. Box 2321, Santa Fe, New Mexico 87504-2321.

Book and Cover design › Vicki Ahl
Body typeface › Minion Pro
Printed on acid-free paper
∞
eBook 978-1-61139-259-3

Library of Congress Cataloging-in-Publication Data

Raciti, James J., 1933-
  [Poems. Selections]
  The bird chart boy : new and selected poems / by James J. Raciti.
    pages cm
  ISBN 978-0-86534-986-5 (softcover : alk. paper)
  I. Title.
  PS3618.A337A6 2014
  811'.6--dc23
                        2014001569

WWW.SUNSTONEPRESS.COM
SUNSTONE PRESS / POST OFFICE BOX 2321 / SANTA FE, NM 87504-2321 /USA
(505) 988-4418 / ORDERS ONLY (800) 243-5644 / FAX (505) 988-1025

*D*edicated to my wife Maryhelen Raciti-Jones with love and respect for her wise counsel, her love of language, and skill in technical matters. She has been devoted to assisting me in bringing my writing to life.

Contents

III. Much Later – New Poems / 87

Introduction

*I*am delighted to write the introduction to my husband James'
third collection of poems. Although I have collaborated with
him for several years providing mainly technical support for
his writing, I have not until now become fully acquainted with
his poetry. I would like to provide the reader with some personal
insights and guidance as to how his development of ideas has
unfolded into *The Bird Chart Boy* which spans a lifetime of events.
The poems are best read sequentially.

Although the poetry taken from the collection *Charles*
appears at the end of this book, it was written in 1959 after the
untimely death of his brother. While studying in France, James
learned that Charles had leukemia. After months of hope that his
remission would continue, Charles unfortunately was overtaken
by his disease and died. In memory of his brother, James began to
write poetry to deal with his loss. He selected the sonnet as a means
of expressing his emotions; the sonnet as a form remote from the
present and formal in style.

The *Bird Chart* Boy begins with the author's reflections on
his early years in Girard College, a private preparatory school for
boys in Philadelphia. James was enrolled in the school at the age
of six and joined his older brother Charles there for the length of
their elementary and secondary studies. The poem "Brothers Line"
reveals the loneliness of young boys separated from home and
family.

The selection of poems taken from *Dabs of Myself,* a work originally published in 1998 covers the years of James' university studies in Grenoble, France; his first marriage and the birth of his children (Charles, Marc and Claudia). The poems also reflect his years as a university professor in both France and Spain. He eventually returned to the states and continued his writing, publishing both fiction and non-fiction.

The "New Poems" in the section "Much Later" cover James' life in his years after retirement. The poem, "No Death for Me" was inspired by his fear and concern for the safety of his son Marc who was serving with the US Army at the time in several war zones. Fortunately Marc was one of the lucky ones to return safely.

As I read through the poems again and again, I discover new tones, shades of language and imagery. For example, the words spoken by the young boy in "First Shower," a poem appearing in the first section, and the old man in "I Heard Them Whispering" in a later section both have the innocent, child-like quality and expression we all may have experienced in referring to our own lives. I encourage you to make similar discoveries as you read the collection.

—Maryhelen Raciti-Jones
January 2014

I

Early – New Poems

Gentle Tapping

Long before my father died
and after I had just turned four
I'd sometimes hear his footsteps

in the dark or standing by the door,
locked for the night. It was Auntie Rose,
I think, who first talked to me of death,

who mentioned that her mother
sleeping by the window, heard a
gentle tapping, which Auntie

hadn't heard. Please open it; they want
to come inside her mother said.
My Auntie then reached up and

pulled the window wide,
helped by a gust which filled
the little room and then rushed

out taking the old woman's life as well.
So that's how death had come,
I think my Auntie said.

A Thousand Years

For a thousand years,
we were children
making tiny circles with

our three-wheeled bikes
on summer sidewalks,
our hands still sticky

from some forgotten
ice cream cone.
For a thousand years,

we played kicked the can,
marbles and stick ball
until the long day, at last

gave up its light
and mothers' voices
added threats to their

repeated calls.

Remembering

At a time so long ago
that even I have pain
remembering,

my mother led me to a
place where
children were at play.

So I played,
with forehead wet and
face puffed out with heat,

and still came back
from time to time,
to where she sat

as though to ask permission
for being just a child.
But soon the all-absorbing chase

took all of my attention.
When I, at last, remembered where
I was and why,

I raced back to the bench
where mother was, but wasn't.
She had gone and left me

in a place where
children were at play.

Only Six

The boy had just turned six
and hadn't yet the mind to understand.
He held the heavy gate tight in his hands

and pressed his head halfway
between the wrought iron bars
to look as far as eyes could see

at where the road bent to the left,
beneath the willow tree.
He could see no further because …

because his new world ended there
beyond the darkness of the tree.
His mother just forgot to say goodbye,

as off she hurried to some pressing matter.
For him, there would be little consolation
in later years to learn

that she, as he, had wept
the first day of his boarding school.
It's true he did expect her to return.

She was his mom and he belonged to her.
Arms loaded down with her purchases
she'd sweep him up and take him home again

where all the love and warmth he knew would be.
She did not come that day, or night or in the morning.

The First Shower

How could he know the soap
would burn his eyes?
Never having had a shower

before, the tub being all
he knew at home; his mother's
soap never used to burn.

And all those strange boys pushing
into him and shouting in
his ears and putting more

soap in his hair, keeping him
from washing off his face.
They were making play

of the new boy. The water from
thirty showers turned hot then cold
as Mrs. G. shouted out commands

like a marshal on parade
certain whose fault the tumult was
and made it clear he would be made

to pay for all the fuss.
It was too much this first day far from home:
the laughing boys, the soap and

tears and burning eyes.
How could he know?

Not a Newby

"Prove you're not a newby
and show me the inside of your belt."
But I was well prepared for being challenged,

having spent the morning rubbing off
the newness against the concrete step,
mixing in some dirt, to make the belt look old

and making sure that I could pass for one of them.
Getting caught would mean a punishment from
Mrs. G. like sitting on the floor and not allowed to

see the movie show but worse to be ridiculed by
the other boys. But a newby I'd still be until another boy
would be admitted to the Hum from beyond those walls.

1943

Bright flashlights in our eyes
and shaken into wakefulness,
we were herded from our beds

and made to walk, one behind the
other into the dark hallways where
we were told to wait. The flashlight

bearers spoke in whispered tones,
lest we overhear and learn the reason
for this midnight rout.

Sit against the walls and be still,
a voice from the darkness said, and
don't fall back to sleep. But we did

doze off because we were only
eight or nine years old and needed sleep.
A voice beside me that I recognized

as Ernie's told me that Tojo was
bombing out the city and soon
would come and take us all away.

And we believed that it could all be true.
We hadn't heard the air raid siren
or the all clear signal and had to take

a grownup's word for it, like we always
had to do since no one ever told us much.

The Bonfire

I never questioned where they
found the crates but there they
were stacked higher than a tree,

ready for the burning sacrifice
of All Hallows Eve.
Seven-year olds invaded from

West End could barely hide their glee
running from the House Group

up to mix with bigger boys and

dance around the fire,
as in some pagan rite.
There wasn't much variety

in dress back in the early forties—
most of us were either
cowpokes or redskins—

Great for whooping it up
as the ritual began. Familiar faces
of folks we knew so well, took on

macabre forms in shimmering flames.
"Now don't get too close or you'll catch on fire."
That was Housemaster Mr. N. we

recognized his voice above the noise; he
never spoke to us without his megaphone.
Several hundred boys had to be watched.

Who could tell what they might do, so wild and
beyond control they had become.

The Infirmary

The children's ward was dimly lit by just
the colored lights of a small fir tree.
Seventeen of us were to remain, too ill

to be allowed the two-week holiday.
Tucked in our beds, we waited quietly
and listened to the carols being sung

somewhere down the hall. A boy told
me, he'd heard it from a nurse that
Santa would drop by and give us each a toy

or maybe just an apple or a fountain pen.
I hoped it wasn't just a rumor that we
often hear at the infirmary.

That morning I was changed from full to liquid diet,
because my temperature had risen two degrees.
I wasn't hungry but I really hoped to get

the ice cream we were promised early in the day.
It was Karl the janitor who came
dressed up in red with beard and all

and gave a stocking full to each of us.
There was an apple and a pen, a small red car
and walnuts and a little book of prayers.

I guess I must have fallen fast asleep
before the ice cream came.

Kind of Authority

What kind of authority is that
to let a boy selected from another class
check our toothbrushes to see if we had

cleaned our teeth? And off he'd go along
the line of basins touching brushes as he went.
What kind of authority is that

to decide who gets punished for
leaving a dry brush in the plastic cup,
as though we could not wet the brush without

putting it in our mouths?
If the govie had to know who brushed and who
had not, let her not delegate this degrading search

but rather let her inspect the teeth and not the brush
of those she suspected of this base offense.

Whirling

Packed in heavy winter coats,
our arms and necks immobilized in
wool against the late November wind,

we knew the four o'clock whistle
soon would sound and send us back
indoors to bowls of steaming milk and

sugar cookies.
All the same, we wanted
to remain with the

wind and darkened sky;
whirling, again whirling with heads
thrown back and eyelids closed

and mouths wide open to catch
on eager tongues the brand new flakes
of falling snow.

The Midnight Train

Even as a child, I found it
hard to fall asleep,
just because someone
told me it was time.

I'd lie awake while all
the beds around me
carried off their charges
into quiet slumber.

I waited just until I knew
the governess had gone to
bed as well. Then I'd wend
my way between the beds to the

bathroom in the hall and lock the door.
Through the window, I could
see the famous wishing star.

Within a moment, I had pressed
the magic button which turned the
bath into my private, midnight train

that connected me to the
basement of my house,
so many miles away, and to all the toys

I was obliged to leave behind.
I found my cowboy suit, my hat
and holster, my magic set

and drums, which thoughtfully
I did not bang for fear of
waking grandpa or our setter, Rex

sleeping in the yard. The midnight
train soon tooted to remind me, I
had to make my journey back again.

Clean Plate Club

The cows are eating garlic, that's what
the govie said when we complained
about the terrible flavor of the milk.

Who were we to complain about the milk?
Her eyes seemed to ask—orphans all.
We could not leave a drop of this milk

in our glasses for wasn't there a war on?
And what about the starving people in the world?
We knew the Chinese were our friends

but not the Japs. I couldn't keep it straight—
they looked so much alike but we could never
mention that to Mrs. G. who scolded us for little reason.

She made us join the clean plate club and throw no
food away so we made a game of shining up
our plates with pieces of our bread to show her

we supported the efforts of the war. Sometimes when
she got mad, she'd dump a bunch of
cauliflower on our plates, just to be mean.

We could always count on Nelson to announce
that his plate was so clean, it didn't need a washing.

The Bird Chart Boy

In class I was the bird chart boy,
could name its thirty-seven birds
and show just how to match a name

with picture, touching with electric poles.
It was for Mrs. Witty's pleasure,
that my chair was placed

next to the chart to protect it
from her wanton boys, bent on using
poles for dueling swords.

I hadn't heard her come behind my desk—
I was so deep into the civics test,
she loved to spring on us.

To peer above my head upon the page,
she tried to move her ample rear
into a space of eight small inches,

between the bird chart and my chair.
The rip was like the shot heard 'round the world.
It was her blue silk dress that caught

the metal hook, that held the poles in place.
The world stood still but
her reaction was swift and punitive—

She slapped the innocent head of the
former bird chart boy.

Bird Chart Boy Returns

I bore no ill for that uncalled for slap
and chalked it up as what some grownups do
when they are out of sorts, as ten-year-olds

always feel they are. I kept my distance from
her swinging arm and stayed as quiet as a mouse.
One day she put aside her books and talked to us of birds.

"We have twenty birdbaths on the campus of the Hum,"
she began, "that need fresh water often during the week.
I wonder if there is a young man in this class willing to

sacrifice his recreation hour to fill ten baths a day."
The silence in the room roared in our ears as all of us
studied something on our fingernails, not daring to look up.

I knew as goalie of our section's soccer team,
no way could I take time to bathe her darling birds.
There was impatience in her voice. "Unless I have a volunteer,

I shall have to pick someone with proven skills to do the job."
Ah, that leaves me out, I thought with a sudden surge of relief.
"James, the job is yours; come see me for details after the class."

Much worse than any slap I could receive was this new indignation,
and the fear that I'd forever be the bird chart boy.

Brothers Line

The week was long and still no word from him—
Sunday always came and brought me hope.
Two hours in the sun we walked.

He gave me good things to eat
and messages from home,
his smile and with it

gave me something
I learned called

Love.

Oh, he cared
and showed me how

to handle difficulties
and grow in harmony with
all and sometimes how to fight,

if fighting had to be. All this my heart held
while I would stand and wait for him to come—
The week was very long and still no word from him.

Detention

The yellow tab was the detention slip.
It carried all the weight and
condemnation of a *lettre de cachet*

for the person whose name was written on it.
It was the falling sword that separated the naughty boy
from his Saturday outing with his family and friends.

Many times I was detained by such a slip of paper
for some forgotten infraction of the govie's rules—
being where I had no right to be, saying what

I had no right to say or doing what was known to be forbidden.
It really was quite easy for a ten-year old
to lose his Saturday privilege by doing what was

very natural to him—to get away with something on the sly.
But never getting caught was the perfect trick.
On a Tuesday afternoon in early May, Mrs. G. wrote me up

and put the slip out on her desk in open view to all.
I'd been tempted once again to test my wits against
the grownups of the school in whose charge we were.

The slip was to be given to Mr. N. by noon on Thursday
prior to the Saturday detention. My task was simple—
just make the yellow slip of paper disappear.

We all knew Mrs. G's memory was
not the best, for wasn't she always calling
us by someone else's name?

I waited until she left the section common room,
then I pushed the slip to the farthest corner of her desk—
out of sight, I thought, therefore out of mind.

My weekend was secure. The list came out on
Saturday morning. And there I saw my name.
I never learned just where my reasoning had failed.

The Grudge Line

Detained on Saturday meant walking
for an hour in the grudge line
around the soccer field until the role

was called and we could disappear
until the role was called again.
The housemaster's trick was to make

it impossible to guess when he'd blow
the whistle and check his list against our
happy faces. Sometimes he wouldn't check

for hours at a time and then, to throw us off,
he'd do it every fifteen minutes, making sure
we wouldn't hop the wall and go to town.

Better minds than ours had devised this plan
as infallible as the Pope himself until...
Mousy Eldman came upon the scene,

a new housemaster who wouldn't know a Nelson
from a Merkelovich, so we were duty bound to
put him to the test.

Each time he blew the whistle, we gave a
different name until he was so perfectly
confused trying to match faces to our names.

At two o'clock we struck. Three of us
hopped the wall while the others covered
us by getting back into the line to give another name.

We bragged and pranced and flaunted our success -
heroes of the class for one whole week until
on Saturday morning dressing for our outing,
we saw our names once more on the detention list.
We weren't getting smarter fast enough.

Good Friends

In the building named Good Friends,
which today exists no more,
lived the boys too young to show
the signs of adolescence,
(though there have been some
notable exceptions)

but too old to want stuffed animals
on their beds. These orphan boys, had
they had a home, would have been of
an age to lock the bathroom door,
leaving mom outside.

Here, at shower time, the boys held
up their trousers until all female presence
had gone to upper floors and
boys would be free to take the showers,
section at a time. The traditional, all-male-on-board

cry was: "Drop Em." Gleefully would thirty-two
bodies shed their clothes and
run into the steamy shower rooms.
Housemasters, some, I now know,
should have gone upstairs as well,

flicked wet towels at tardy tails
to get them running faster.
Sometimes, a boy would fall—
tripped or stumbled, who could say?
But the rough cemented floors would

guarantee more care next time and
greater speed.

Radio Shows

How could a bunch of ten-year olds
behave the whole day long?
To be allowed to listen

to the programs on the radio
after the time for lights out—
the rules were clear—we must behave.

The section's devotees of
Captain Midnight and *Baby Snooks*
would try to keep the rest of us

in line, early in the day
but they never managed to
succeed that well.

We relied, therefore,
on mercy and understanding
from the governess.

Thirty-two of us in section ten
were not so bad—just noisy and
excited, as the govie used to say.

One hour before lights out,
we'd at last come to our senses
and quiet down. Mrs. G. would

roll the radio out into the dorm,
turn out the lights and tune us in to
THE FBI IN PEACE AND WAR,

reminding us to wash with Lava soap.
We squealed quietly in our beds
as we listened...

Confession

Roman Catholics had petitioned
that their boys be now allowed
to say confession and attend the

weekly Mass beyond the granite
confines of the School.
Not a thrilling perspective was it for

the nine-year-old sinners who,
with the joy of buying stale and broken
doughnuts for five cents a bag

at the local bakery, had to catalog their
sins for some old priest to hear.
Coupled with the joy for an hour's

escapade outside the Hum
was the fear that what
they might confess would

bring down the wrath of God and
priest upon their heads.
In solemn lines outside the

dark confessional, the boys would
plan the way they might confess
truth enough to gain some

absolution and yet not quite enough
to have the priest initiate
a full-blown interrogation.

The Confessional

"Bless me father, for I have sinned."
Now what could these young children
say that would be of any interest to the

Church? But in their minds they had a
plan to use up the time by slowly
itemizing silly sins and then gloss over

quickly ones they feared to tell.
"I have disobeyed my governess
and lied more often than I can count.

I have been angry and impatient..."
The priest knew that game and was waiting
for the meaty stuff. Then quickly the kids would add,

"I've been unclean in thought, word and deed."
"Ah," said the priest, "was the unclean deed only
with yourself or with another?"

The darkness of the booth would
hide his smile, the only pleasure
he would get in hearing sins!

II

Later – Selected Poems
from
Dabs of Myself

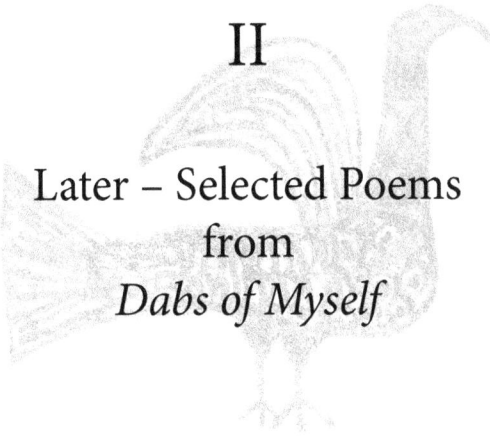

A Terrible Thing

A terrible thing to hear the doctor say
the birth went well but your son's right foot—
It's not quite right. How could I wake his
mother with this news, after twenty terrible

hours filled with agony?
There it was. My first born handicapped at birth
by some cruel twist. And twist it was,
to everyone's relief. Yes relief that bad positioning

had merely turned the foot around. Had I let
doctor finish his remarks, I would have learned
that simple stretching and massage would bring
the foot back into line and lying flat but

we had to take these measures now at once before
the soft muscles and sinews of his foot were set.

I Never Learned

I never learned the proper way
to be a father, having lost my
own before my days at school.

And yet, as little persons gathered
around me, I learned from them the
things they needed most.

At this writing, they are grown and gone.
I can no longer dress them hurriedly for school
or tell them stories, firing up their minds

put daily in my trust.
I never learned the way to set examples,
so imperfect was my life in many ways.

I can't even say I did my best for them,
so busy with my own life, I had become.
The time's at hand to draw the line of reckoning,

adding all that's good, then all the rest.
If there's any satisfaction in my failures,
it's that my children too one day may fail this test.

Isla de Formentera

There was a time, I'm sure
you had great satisfaction in
keeping Formentera for

yourself— your way of
getting back at me for
dismissing you.

What you'll never know is
that deep within my heart and
mind, I have it all.

All I need to do is close my eyes
and I can walk every inch of
the island house, feel the cool

Spanish tile on the soles of my
feet, still hot and sandy from the beach.
I walk the roof at night with my head upturned

to a multitude of stars, which protect themselves
from view in busy towns. Still with
eyes firmly shut, I see mile after mile of stone

walls that farmers built to clear their fields for
cultivation, roads are as the Romans saw them,
when they planted wheat from which the island

takes its name. Roads still rough to keep tourists
from venturing close. And then the sea! How
jealously each segment will protect its own

shade of blue, or green or violet taking turns to
change with private deals cut with the hour of the
day, with the wind and the omnipresent sun.

Dusty

I didn't like the way my car got
dusty down below in the garage so I
brought it to the living room which made

my wife complain that it should not be there.
Though it was difficult, I moved the car up
the staircase to the master bedroom and put

it by the bed, where it would be dust free
and close at hand, but I kept bumping into it
as I got up so often during the night.

So I folded up the car as best I could
and brought it to the bathroom where
I could bathe it as I bathed myself.

Now the car began to grunt that I was
getting soap into all its parts, which
put the windshield wipers into constant motion.

Disgusted with it all, I pulled the plug
and watched my auto circle the drain and then
go down and disappear from sight.

In Full Revolt

Again the crimson clouds turned dawn to morning—
but I ignore my ringing clock.
I feel the shower on my neck and shoulders,
although I am still nestled in my bed.
Again, I am in full revolt and plan
to sleep away the day;
but then through cross-woven lashes, I see
my shoes leaving for work without me.

No Friends

I have no friends
it is clear;
nor do I want

a single one!
If there are men
about me,

I want to push them down
beneath my feet.
If there are women,

beneath my waist
will do.

When Pregnant Women

When pregnant women fall
husbands shout, "Hon...ney" when
they really mean to say "Oh shoot!"
And husbands' mothers roll their eyes and
shoot horned fingers to the ground.

When pregnant women fall,
a hundred crickets cease their song and
two-year olds hand mom the ball because
she's now just their size with knees splayed
wide in her new game.

When pregnant women fall
nothing really comes of it.

La Sagrada Familia

From my balcony, I can see
the spires of the Sagrada Familia
still rising in its local controversy.
What was once genius has
become guilt, tacked to coat lapels
by tiny fingers once a year.
Who would refuse to give so that construction
might continue as Gaudi once proposed?
Is this not like motherhood and *pan bagnat*
for Catalans? Having taken the wrong turn, they
prefer to drive around the world just
to prove they've made the right decision.

One Would Think

One would think with all those weddings bands
tossed away by disenchanted brides
that I'd have found at least just one.

One would think with all the plates and crystal
from bridal showers, thrown
against the wall by angry husbands,
they'd have only take-out cartons left.

One would think that all the brains and common sense
flowing from their bodies during their mating romps
that they'd have nothing left to pass on to the kids.

But they're still tossing rings and things and romping
to exhaustion and we're all still here.
One would think.

Civil War

From north of the border
word was spread
by traveling tourists
that civil war had come again
to Spain.
The streets of Barcelona
were on fire,
explosions filled the air
piercing screams from
little children added to the madness
and confusion.
How eager was the outside world
to call by other names,
the games of
San Juan's Eve.

El Diagonal

Below the pensive stare of Verdaguer,
the Barcelona traffic cop
sends us moving beneath his swinging
arms, never looking down
to see how near we pass.

Then at some silent, distant trumpet sound,
he goes to change the movement of the game,
tossing back his cape and lifting pen
and pad above his head,
he moves in for the kill.

Paseo de Gracia

At the corner of the street,
he stepped into my view,
with head thrown back
and shoulders squared,
he hurried like a busy banker

to some scheduled meeting
of the board. But how could I know?
He did not tell me who he was,
but from his torn and slept-in clothes,
and laceless shoes,

I was not surprised to
see him reach
full arm's length
into the rubbish can
for the news of the day.

There She Is

There she is
sitting on the far side
of my closed eyes
waiting for me to
open business
for the day.

She rattles her milk bottles
at me and stands first on one foot
and then the other, impatiently.
She has business with me I
presume but I will still
ignore her.

When my work is finished
for the day, she is still there
wanting to know if
there is still time
for one thing or another
before closing.

You Were Lonely

You were lonely so you ran a stick
against the bars of my cage.
My yellow eyes looked back

at you in anger but then
I turned away. You were lonely
so you held out something good to eat,

catching my attention,
doing what it was in my dark corner.
I watched you pace back and forth, wanting

to come in and not wanting to, both
curious and afraid. Seeing you this way
infuriated me. I threw things at you

to drive you off and made such awful
sounds. I pounded on my chest, then
on the walls but you still remained.

You listened to my noises
and tried to find some harmony
in them. You stayed until...

until you were quite certain
I had learned you were free
to come and go and I was not.

Distracted

The chain of our encounters
had been snapped.
Distracted for a moment

by some trivial thing,
you stepped into a cab
and sped away,

before we had agreed
on time and place when
next we'd meet.

Waiting for this chance,
the city rushed into the void
and in a moment, dared the world
to prove that you and I had
ever been at all.

It Just Slipped Out

It just slipped out— a prayer that
I had so relied on as a child.
Perhaps the moment had been right
for such an unexpected plea.

Had I traveled not a single step since
my days at school when I met each
new obstacle with an entreaty
to the Lord for His intercession?

It just slipped out but I caught
myself in time. How could I have
been so totally deceived?
To think someone important

in the clouds would hear
the quiet whispers of a child,
small in his bed among so many
placed, side by side in that enormous hall.

It gave me peace, although I have none now
to know someone important was in charge
to make my worries disappear and let me
face another day erect and unafraid.

My days of childhood now are far behind.
I have today as much control of life as I had
when off to play I'd go, not thinking that
someday I'd almost let a prayer slip out.

I Am Weak

When I tell you
I am strong, you sneer
and refuse to listen.

When I tell you
I am weak,
you smile and
pester me for more details.

When I tell you
that you're strong,
you invite me in for dinner

so that I can also tell your friends.
When I do, you love me and
I know that I am weak.

St. Valentine

Let the world pay homage to this man
of whom today we know so very little
and what we know has been so banally
proclaimed that we do injury, not honor to
his name. Today for me is like a day ago
when I said how very dear you were to me.
No heart-shaped sweets or flowers do I bring
but simply what I am and how I strive to better be.
Yet all my imperfections may be preferred
to annual onslaughts of chocolate and such
but I have erred before in things I do
and this may not be how I best please you.

Fakespeare

Shall I compare you to a winter's day?
You are more frigid from your place on high.
As you walk by, the blossoms fade away
and winter winds turn gray the summer sky.
Sometimes you stoop to smile at those below
but only if this gesture earns you time
to see how you can profit by this show,
or leap upon their backs to further climb.
But your eternal winter shall not fade
and everything you touch will turn to frost.
For this is how you yourself you made
and the loveliness of life to you is lost.
I could be wrong and you can prove me so
by joining me for dinner and a show.

One Good Thought

I begin each day with one good thought;
I wrap it up and rush it out to you.
You pretend both interest and awe,

then ask me to undo the wrap.
You look at it and say,
Yes, why not? And nothing more.

I beg to know what's really
in your mind. You smile but never
do you speak. And later in the day,

should I see my thought on some
abandoned heap, I forget who put it there
or that ever it was mine.

The Dream Came Back

That dream came back again this night,
and I find it hard to tell you how I feel.
First it is relief—I'm in a safer place

but then will come regret that I still am.
How is it that the thunder of my shouts
did not disturb the woman at my side?

Or was the thunder only in my dream
turned quickly off the moment I awoke?
I wanted so to have some calm return

but knew I was afraid to fall asleep
for fear I'd once again be thrown
into a world of torment and of dread.

What is this sin that in the dark of night
possesses me? What is this nameless guilt?
In daylight I stand tall among all men,

have earned respect and lead where many follow.
The dream I have is painful, raw and rough.
The comfort of my bed is not enough.

Lost

Sometimes I crawl so far
within myself, taking turn
after turn where the outside light

grows dim inside the narrow
passages still unknown to me.
At once, the path will fall away;

then, suddenly I'm plodding
upward until I am completely lost.
And there I'll sit until my breath returns

and I wonder why I've done it once again.
I reach up along the sides

of these walls and find them clammy
like my hands just before I wipe
them on my trouser leg as

someone reaches out to me.
Should some voice make its
way into my hiding place,

it comes in muffled and indistinct—
not meant for me at all.
Sometimes I'd hear my name

and wonder if they can see me.
I keep as quiet as I can, hoping
they will go away. I never know how

I'll make it back again but I do. Then I see
the smiling faces all around as though I've
swum the Channel or won the Triple Crown.

Something Wonderful

Each day
I find myself
waiting for letters or
telephone calls or for
something wonderful
to happen.

Each day,
long before it's over
I decide that I've
mistaken the date and
go about my life
waiting for
tomorrow.

Proof

You said I had to
prove my love and
so I scratched your back

and ran my little finger
in your ear. Then I asked you but
wasn't satisfied until

you quit your job,
sold your home and
packed your children off

to boarding school and
stood before me
naked and alone.

Who Needed Wearing

He brushed away the chalk
from his lapel and sleeve
but left more dust than he removed.
His suit—his wedding suit
was much too dark for class.
He wore it though, just to please his wife
and because it needed wearing.

His briefcase bulged
with uncorrected copies
that he could not take home
though it would please his wife.
The house was much too
full of children
who needed wearing.

That Stare

Whose are those eyes
staring so intently at me?
I'd say there is something

familiar in his face but
no, the coloring is wrong.
The eyelids droop and
the flesh is loose

around his chin.
Whose are those eyes
staring at me so?

He's sure to know it's rude to
lock his eyes on mine
demanding my attention?

I try to walk away, then he turns.
Quickly, I return
and he is there.

I try to start a
staring match, fun at first
but then oddly threatening.

The large brown eyes would not
leave mine alone. My tears
made it that much harder

to defend myself against
that dominant, dark brown
Irish setter's stare.

The Metro

Here again is the
smell of tired people—
old from a day of work

within the city,
folded faces against
this strange intimacy,

as unconcerned with the stale
news of the day as with
their own spent moments

when washed away in rings
on their faces at
bedtime.

They consult the hour
on their wrists
more from habit

than interest,
at each loud hiss
of the heavy metal doors.

He Didn't Shave

Today I saw the man I feared
I might become.
He didn't shave or
change the clothes
he'd slept in during the night.
No work had he to do or place
to go except the park where
those too old or those too young
wonder why he's there.
Had he not some meeting to attend?
Were there no important papers
to be signed?
"Will you let me throw the ball?"
a voice deep within him said
to a group of little children.
They looked up from their game
at his runny nose and weepy eyes
then moved their game farther down
the path.

Via Augusta

There is a little park I know
where sometimes I will go and sit.
One day, while sitting on my bench,

I saw a most exquisite girl go by.
I looked.
My look at her was such

as to make the ladies sitting near and far
tug modestly at their skirts.

You Did

You said you'd come
to spend the night
and lay your body next to mine.

You did. You said you'd read
aloud your verses and
ask to hear my own.

You did.
You said you'd drop
your clothing in the dark

and slip between the sheets
close to me. You did.
I didn't.

The Ramblas

On the Ramblas
a taxi driver's full range
of emotion
can be had for a five peseta tip
one way
or the other.

Barcelona

Here, nothing misses its chance
at usefulness.
In the absence of brooms and baskets,

white communion dresses
sweep the Sunday streets
while tax collectors—

those armies of small children
shake collection cans at you.

With Dignity

You wanted love
with dignity
and didn't like

my tearing at your
clothes in public.
So I stopped.

You hated how
I loved my beer
and thought

tisane was much
more dignified.
I ordered it.

You criticized my hair,
my clothes, the work I do.
And what you really didn't like

was that small part of you
that chased me shamelessly
by day and night.

Our Mistake

I stood closely
within a ring of people
big and small

watching the animals
in their cages,
when suddenly

a tiny hand reached up
and took my own to hold.
So we stood

holding hands for a while
until, realizing
our mistake,

we broke apart.

Shut in Again

I've been out of work
for thirteen weeks—
hardly long enough to be
concerned about.

Like some extended holiday, except
my mind is working overtime
with plans to get myself
shut in again.

Each day I run along the beach,
my toes dig out wet holes of sand and
the wind chills my face and chest.
It's really wonderful except—

My mind is working overtime
with plans to get myself
shut in again.

Résumé

You asked about my looks.
By Anglo-Saxon standards,
I am short, although more than
half the world looks up to me.

I am heavier by several pounds
than my height in inches
should permit. I hate
most photographs of me

that others like. The ones I like
don't look like me at all.
Current fashion finds
my head too *déplumé*.

Brown eyes—big and somewhat sad,
are good at being seen but
rather worthless in the task
of seeing.

My voice is rich and melodious.
I can be counted on to join in singing
any barroom song.

Being Unemployed

I lied again today and
told a friend about a job,
I did not have—

about a salary
I did not make,
about a business trip

I could not take.
Being unemployed,
I have the best of chances

to turn again to my writing.
But do I do this? Not I.
When I was working at some

senseless task for which
I was being paid,
I had no time to give to my art.

Now I have no art to give
to my time.

You Sent Me Home

I begged to see you but you
had little time for me.
Instead you showed me a book,

told me you knew the author well.
He had slept at your table and
eaten where no food was served.

Between the pages, you had
pressed his tongue still
flapping as we looked at it.

The words he formed moved
like ants across the page.
I confessed I had no book

to give you, so you
sent me home.

Haircut

Getting a haircut and having
a tooth extracted have about the
same level of dread for me.

First of all, I have no favorite
barbershop. They are equally horrid.
Their magazines depress me long before

I get invited to the chair. Seeing how profusely
I've begun to sweat, the barber talcs my
neck and ears and asks me what I'd like,

as though a ham on rye could be an option.
No matter what I say, the barber cuts the way
she damn well pleases. On automatic cut control,

she chops away, her mouth
never ceasing to run on about the most
intimate matters of her life to

the barber in the adjacent chair. Being ignored,
I just relax until she turns to me.
"Where are you from?" She asks, as though she cared

a fig but her question startles me and I have
no easy response, having moved twenty-two times
in the past ten years searching for whatever.

"Oh just around," I say, hoping she doesn't feel obliged
to query any further in her quest for a proper tip.
She quickly flashes the mirror across my neck

so I can view the back. I ask apologetically if she has
found the hairs I store behind my ears that I can never see.
Her eyes are like an angry stamping foot. I had challenged

her ability. Never mind I say and get up from the chair.
My tip is so much larger than she has deserved
but I need to make a clean escape with the
determination—no haircut will I ever get again.

The Merchant's Prayer

I've always been a decent Christian,
regularly attended services at church,
would give my tithes up willingly
and feared Almighty God.

Please give me the strength Oh Lord
to find new ways to further build
my profits so that I can better
serve Thee.

I admit to all that through my prayers
to you, I learned to give up making estimates
for car repairs at my shop and insist that
all customers pay a diagnostic fee—

guaranteed seventy dollars—
however slight the repair. My son
the plumber now sends out two
apprentice workmen to do a job

instead of one so he can charge
a double fee. All this we owe to your
constant guidance but we still have need for more.
Please show us how we can meet your demands
on us. Amen

Chaflans

A nuisance are the chaflans in
this city, for those on foot
find their steps are multiplied
just walking square to square.
Cornered streets are clipped to give
delivery trucks ample space to unload
their wares in clouds of dust,
each time the workmen bounce their
crates upon the sidewalks.
Woe to the car, left there by error
from the night before. It will receive
a sturdy kick or find its side mirrors bent
by workmen's anger. Unless their
attention has been drawn by a passing
lady's ankle.

Albert Speer

A haggard man, not yet old but
spent from years of penance in Spandau
for being brighter than he should

have shown. He did not hold out
his hand at our meeting but
humbly nodded with his head.

Twenty years had taught him
that a proffered hand could be easily
ignored. His home in Heidelberg

had been let out to the winning team
and now he had returned to reclaim it
with what was left of a ruined life.

My colleague Johnny M. would
have to find another house to rent.
Then Johnny had a bright idea. It

was the end of May—the annual
university graduation— a wonderful
event filled with gaiety, attended by

graduates and families as well as
dignitaries. So he invited Speer
perhaps to cheer him up.

That year Henry Cabot Lodge
attended with the soon-to-be
disgraced former governor of
Maryland. More importantly the
Chancellor of West Germany had come,
saw the face of his old enemy, and

whispered something to our dean and
president.
Seeing this Albert Speer
turned and left the hall, where he knew

he had no right to be and wondered
how soon the head of Johnny M.
would roll for such a monumental gaffe.

I Count Myself

I count myself among the
very fortunate who have seen
many of the great treasures of Europe.

The only way I'd tear myself
from a collection, a museum or
a magnificent city was to believe

that life was long and I 'd someday return.
What luxury it would be to walk again
the ancient Roman city beneath

the streets of Barcelona; to hurry
with the German students after
class to the Alte Pinakothek

or to see collections of tapestries
from the kings of France. Will I
once again see the murals of

Fra Angelico on the walls of
the monastery he called home?
I count myself among the

very fortunate to be alive today
to call forth memories of what
I've seen and felt and lived.

Tripoli

My business took me once again to
Tripoli just when Gaddafi came to
power. The rolling southern sea

hadn't changed at all and I could see
that the pristine beaches were yet
to learn how nearby supermarkets
could defile them. An Italian who had
made his home here begged me to
take his savings to deposit with a bank

in Rome before the new regime
took his home, his money and everything
else he owned. All this he said in tears as

he struck with a bamboo pole the dates from
an overhanging palm so we could taste
their sweetness with his wine, grapes and bread.

Asmara

I looked up at the high desk; the smiling
black face of the magistrate hid the anger
he was about to reveal. "You have been

arrested for bearing arms in the city of
Asmara." His English was perfect so I could
not ask him to repeat, although my face did

show confusion. "That sword," he went on.
"Where did you get it?" I smiled as I understood,
the magistrate was referring to a rusty battle sword,

I had within the hour bought from a street merchant.
My smugness wiped the smile off his face as he went
on to explain that Ethiopian ceremonial swords are

weapons, although not of mass destruction. He briefly
enjoyed his little joke but his smile frightened me,
as he demanded to see the receipt for my purchase.

I had no such evidence for a simple twenty-five dollar
souvenir. I tried to smile but that was a mistake.
"You scoff at our laws and will show this sword to your

American friends and say how primitive we are."
My neck was stiff from holding my head at this awkward
angle. I put on a penitent face and hoped for the best.

"You will pay the bursar one hundred American dollars for
this infraction." The gavel came down with finality.
When I returned to my rental car, I found the door forced

open, my briefcase gone as well as the small car radio.

Poet Laureate

At thirty-five thousand feet above
the earth, Dickey nudged me as the
beverage cart came down the aisle.

"I'm buying—get a double for yourself."
Still the bully. He made it clear to me
that he was the closest this country would

come to naming a Poet Laureate.
Still we had no deal for a commencement
speech, though Heidelberg in May seemed

quite attractive. Money, not a degree
was what he wanted most of all,
after Jack Daniels.

Michener

At a lunch given in his honor,
James Michener stuffed his
mouth with food, which gave him

ample time to find an answer.
"Would he help a young talented
writer get started?" Pointing to his

cheeks and chewing still, he
finally said, "Hell no! If he's
any good he'll make it on his

own. Besides, he probably
thinks that already he's a better
writer than I could ever be."

III

Much Later – New Poems

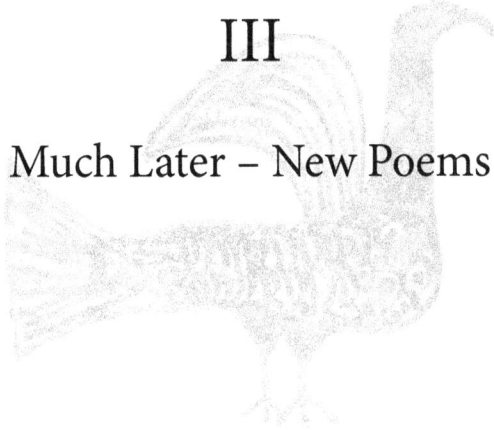

The Son Remembers

Father, tell me once again
the way you took my hand and
led me down the dusty lane
beyond the cala to the shiny sea.

Tell me once again
the way you made me sing
to make the path easier to walk
for little feet.

Eight o'clock was not too
late to take another swim
so often you would say.
Today as I myself have

children of my own with
little feet, I'd like so much
to have you take me once again
down the dusty lane

beyond the cala
to the shiny sea.
But for you, eight o'clock
has come and gone

and the only voice I hear
from you is deep within
the channels of my mind.

Not Too Old

I'm not too old today, not
like last week, when walking through
the park, I became invisible to everyone,
despite my nodding head and cheerful smile.

I'm not too old today, not
like last night, when wobbling
from my bed, I turned into a closet
where the bathroom used to be.

I'm not too old today, not
like this morning, I awoke, at ten to two,
was fully finished with my sleep and
could think of nothing more to do.

I'm not too old today,
to open up my wardrobe, and take
out the clothes I haven't worn in years
to see old shoes, half worn by better feet.

I've kept them all because I can't yet admit
I'll never wear them when I'm younger than today.

I Awoke This Morning

I awoke this morning
with a song upon my lips
quite despite myself for

I had no reason to sing out.
And if later questioned I would
have certainly denied it but

all the same, I broke into
an old familiar melody—
just like that!

Were it not for the cough
that shook me into silence,
I might have sung all day.

Sudden Snow

My neighbor asked if he could plow away
the snow, packed solidly against my door.
I barked my youngest laugh and said
I knew how, in the early spring,
snow melted long before it caused us much concern.

He didn't see the young strong man in me
that I refused to bury in the past.
Instead he wished to help the man he saw—
stringy white-gray hair crushed by a woolen cap,
mismatched sweats, two days of growth upon my cheeks

and darting eyes with spectacles that magnified confusion.
I continued talking to my shovel, then to my hands, rough
and raw from the cold. When I looked up, my neighbor
had gone into his house.

Something Useful

Mostly I'm alone;
and one would think there's
something useful to be learned

about oneself.
But let me tell you
how it worked with me.

I never learned a single thing
on how to organize my day,
or be a better neighbor or

know what's true from false.
Because you see
I never would permit myself

to be alone with me.
The moment I would enter
my front door, I'd fill my

home with outside sounds
of radio or TV.
And then I'd grab the nearest

book and pretend to read.
Being mostly all alone,
I never gave myself the time

for conversation.

Four Boats

Four boats for Carlos
I can remember
of the years I've lived so far.

The first was brightly colored vinyl,
that I inflated with an anxious breath
and I sat you down with all

your plastic toys.
The second, as a young man,
you lost your boat at sea and with it all the

carelessness of youth and almost life itself.
The next came quickly on its heels.
It was a gift from me to make you feel

you still could be a sailor in my trust.
And now the fourth,
oh yes the fourth.

You didn't tell me of it;
you bought it on your own
but never wanted me to know.

It was your boat that you
would only share with those
you love.

No Death for Me

No death for me while going
north to Baghdad. A bit too
smart I was to let them take
me down. But not so for my

buddies—Reese, Guillermo
and Ranelli. They took a rapid
passage home to tearful families
amid press microphones.

Bro Reese may not have known,
though born within the city,
not to let a toothless, smiling
stranger get too close.

So up they went, black and
brown, arm in arm, like lovers.
His scabbing new tattoo melted
on his chest. I guess Guillermo

never saw the need to read a map.
He turned his humvee right but
wrong yes right into hands that
took his uniform and drained the

kindness of his heart into the desert sand.
Dino Ranelli fell asleep when he should not have.
But briefly, he awoke beneath a storm of lead.
Then with a grin, he went to sleep again,

having nothing more, at that moment he could do.
But I'm much too smart to let them take me down.
I knew that "free the people from
oppression" really meant,

fun at late night parties to celebrate

the winning of a bid, a contract to
rebuild a city broken in despair.
All this I've learned just now—but

had no notion of before a sniper's
bullet made my glasses jump.
I also know that several weeks
from now, in splendid evening dress,

they'll lift their bubbling glasses high
to toast the dead but do they know
that so reluctantly had we fought,
we warriors whose options were

so limited at birth? Before dividing
up the spoils of our success, these
makers of the rules will toast the
heroes who gave away their lives—

among the names will be Bro Reese,
Guillermo and Ranelli and
of course, they'll mention me.

Seasons

I love you now as always
you desired, with coolness
in my southern hemisphere.
How annoying it must have

been for you to struggle for
so long beneath my ardent urgencies.
I must admit the change I see in
me is restful. No longer do I center

duties of the day around that drive,
which always left me breathless and forlorn.
Now that winter has come to stay,
I am in peace. In peace, except for the

flowering springtime I see in you,
both hemispheres in vibrant bloom.
Your hair, your nails, your slimming
waist and the softness of your skin,

all give me pause to presume that
in a year or two, you'll invite your
girlfriends to the house
for slumber parties.

Stubble

Sometimes I awake to a world
where nothing seems to please me.
Today it was the stubble of

a beard that I had carefully
scraped away just yesterday.
Here it was again, daring me to

have another go at it. Perhaps I will
and then again perhaps I won't.
It's fashionable of late for young men

to leave a little shadow for that virile
look. With me, the gray pops out and
passersby look to where they may
drop a coin for me.

It's Harder Now

It's harder now each day
to make myself presentable.
My hair is thin and gray and

no longer garnishes my top but pokes
itself from all the strangest places.
Although my smile shows

now the great success of
modern dentistry, should I
expand this smile, it shows

the battlefield where my budget lost
its fight with my insurance.
As a lad of seventeen, I would neglect

myself in the most unsavory ways;
yet, I had found myself surrounded
by much pleasant company.

I'd often wear a shirt I'd slept in
for a while or having no clean socks,
I'd wear the ones that shocked

my senses least.
I'd just make no attempt to
make myself presentable.

And yet ... Today,
I try so very hard.

I Sometimes Wonder

I sometimes wonder what I miss the most,
as the years pile up in stacks upon my back.
Of course I miss the people who were near

who saw my infant yawns as awesome feats.
Their faces will live on in me,
for yet a little while.

I also miss the places that have moved away or
hidden themselves inside some shopping mall.
What happened to the drinking trough

that thirsty horses gathered to?
Majestically it stood alone in the middle
of our largest avenue.

And in regret, I'll always miss the better way
that things got done, with honesty and care.
And how each merchant would take pride to give

full measure of his wares or expertise.
I sometimes wonder what I miss the most.
Perhaps I'll never know. It may be my undirected youth.

Voraciously I'd feed a body full of needs
but took so little time to think
or wonder.

Déjà

The world's become déjà
quite strange to me.
Faces I have known have
changed their form.

In every sentence I hear
words I never heard before—
confusing words that have metallic ring.

We don't communicate as
once we did. I send my son a letter
and expect one in return but
get instead a hurried cell phone

call made from his car
between Electronic World
and the shopping mall—
That's two full minutes of
distracted talk.

The world's become déjà
quite strange to me.
I no longer own the tools
with which to fix my car.

Even the simple radio won't
work unless it's programmed
to perform. I wouldn't dare swim
at the public beach for I haven't

yet agreed to have my back scraped clean
of hair. The world's become déjà quite
strange to me. At first I tried to keep apace
with changes as they came

but they left me far behind. My camera,
my watch and then my phone
would not cooperate as I was
accustomed that they should.

His Best Work

I wonder if He'll ever try again,
having botched His first attempt at
making me. Perhaps He'll attach a

sign to my back, to warn all others off.
"Not in my Image." It might say or
"Spoiled Ingredients. Please Destroy."

If we both agree that I am not His best work,
let's examine one who, by a common definition,
is successful. His voice is loud at Sunday services.

His business thrives; his stomach pushes out with pride,
as he makes his way through the crowd of admirers.
Everyone is as sure of him as he is of himself.

I wonder if He is proud of this one
or will He want to try again.

The Presidential Seal

The first thing he requested
when he came into
the White House was

to see the Presidential Seal.
He'd heard the seal was
everywhere, and thought seeing it

would be fun. He imagined
what a sad surprise
its sudden demise would be

if they had to scrape its
tattered body free from
the bottom of the
Secret Service barge.

The Favorite Son

Annoying signs were
everywhere why had it taken
us so long to see? His antics were

far more than we could bear,
his intelligence below a passing grade.
Yet we asked him to return.

This bush did not
burn brightly enough to lead
the other nations, much less our own

though someone had convinced him
he was heaven's choice to throw his
bright beam of faith into the dark corners

of the heathen world.
This lad had brought fresh fish
to feed the Presidential Seal,

had promised Mexico a disappearing
border, had turned his cabinet into fools,
and destroyed the reputations of at least

four world leaders.
It should have been a clue to us -
Fresh fish?

Waiting

Waiting for the traffic light
to change, I had a simple
thought. Since younger

people have much more time
at their disposal in the
remaining span of life
and conversely, older folks

must have much less,
there ought to be a traffic light
of shorter wait, for seniors.
Well...maybe not.

Hiding

Because Noche follows me
from room to room,
and from floor to floor

throughout the day,
I thought it might be fun
to run up the stairs

and hide in a bedroom closet.
There in the dark I wait until my
legs get tired. I peep through the

crack in the door, but the cat is nowhere
to be found. I suppose some alluring scent
has sent her off her course.

The Plastic Spoon

It wasn't where I'd always put it,
beside the faucet near the sago palm.
That's what I get for letting her dry
and put away the dinner plates.
Just an ordinary plastic spoon,
you ask? Yes, advertised as Old English

Country White, in a package of forty-five.
I looked in the drawer where silverware is
kept, it wasn't there. Surely, I could take

another one from the pack but that is not the
point. This spoon is the one I always use to
dish out Noche's food. It had many weeks of

faithful service yet to perform.
I really hate to have my day upset
this way. I stopped in my tracks

and listened. I thought I heard the spoon
cry out from inside the canister of
fish flakes. No it wasn't there. My wife

is happily at work not thinking how
annoying this has been for me.
Could it have been thrown away or sent down

the disposal by some carelessness?
I opened up the trash bag and there it was—
broken in two by someone using it

as it was not meant to be used.
At least she could have told me.

The Petition

I had it planned for the early morning,
with a sturdy box to stand on at a busy
intersection where the cars would stop
when the traffic light turned red.

I wondered why it hadn't been
addressed before, more important
this was than many silly petitions
we learn about each day.

There'd be a meeting for all those who
thought as I, who wanted to make changes
in our lives. How could it not appeal to
everyone?

We needed signatures for sure but it wasn't
clear to me as yet where I'd send these names.
Demanding a stop to aging is not a simple issue.

The Proffered Finger

I've trained the cat not to ignore my
proffered index finger. For to do so
she might miss the taste of something sweet.

From clear across the room I would point
and she would come a running to inspect
what treasure I might have.

Sometimes it would be a bit of cream dipped from
my own dish or the tip of a Hershey candy kiss but
most of all Noche loved the taste of peanut butter.

I knew I could not treat myself
without first treating her.
If ever I'd forget, I'd feel her cold persistent glare
from far across the room.

The Gated Community

It was a neighborhood I hadn't
seen before. Somewhat distracted,
I had let the car turn where

it would. Behind a wall I saw
upscale homes, far beyond
my means, the gate guards,

decked out in bright red uniforms
and broad smiles, held up their hands
to prevent me from entering.

"This is by far the most extraordinary
development I have ever seen!" I
mumbled in my defense for having

tried to trespass and I asked who lived
beyond these walls. The guards smiled,
answering in unison: "Just those whose

lives have given them everything they
could imagine. Drive away. Forget you've
ever come this way."

Coleridge

When I first read Coleridge's *Dungeon,*
I was only twenty-three and could have wept
at the innocence of his premise—Let criminals

out of their dungeons so that they no longer be
"a jarring and dissonant thing." The goodness of
the world around them would absorb their evil intents.

Like *The Lime Tree Bower My Prison* and *Kubla Khan,*
Coleridge lived in a world of his own making. Today,
he'd be far to the left of the most progressive New

Englander. I read the *Dungeon* again last night
and found myself far to the right of Kubla Khan.

Albrecht Dürer

Why did Albrecht Dürer feel the need
to copy the engraving of Andrea Mantegna—
Battle of the Sea Gods? Was it in admiration

of the Italian's art? Was it to prove that
he, a German from Nuremburg, could do
in fewer strokes and less time what Mantegna

had achieved the year before? His trip
to Italy, especially Venice gave Dürer's work
a finer quality, a softer touch as he exhibited in his

self portrait— one in which he paints himself as a
member of the nobility— carelessly detached.
His version of *The Battle of the Sea Gods* is

less defined but one could say he gives the sea and
sky a more natural appearance, the scales and faces
of the gods— are much less menacing in design.

For those who care.

Living

He had just celebrated his one
hundred years of life but for
a long time he'd felt the pressure

he was occupying valuable space.
He took to hiding away from others,
as though, he might escape their

condemnation. For twenty years or
more, he believed it was bad luck to
appear in public as though to flaunt

his good fortune and so end the life he
had become so eager to maintain.
He had been careful not to let the

government know his whereabouts,
took no retirement or Medicare and
maintained no social security number.

His moving from city to city had been
frequent, he paid only in cash and owned
no credit card. He had taken to changing

his appearance with wigs, dark glasses
and hats. He had no family or friends or
church. He could easily survive on just a

handful of bread or rice and drank only
water from the tap. He never asked
himself why he wanted to live on but
this was all he knew.

Their Way

William said he wet the bed again last night because he
was so frightened of the dark.
How patiently they tried to

teach him how to hold the railing
of the bed and walk, one foot before
the other until the brightness of the

hallway lamp would show him where the
bathroom was, but...
William wet the bed again because he

hadn't learned as yet to do it
their way though he knew so well
how scolded he would be

especially by his daughter-in-law.

I Heard Them Whispering

I heard them whispering
behind the door
and strained my ears to

listen to their words.
I had become too difficult
she said to keep at home

and that I would be more
comfortable at Belle.
Had I not awoke to use the bath,

I never would have heard
them talk of this. My son would
come to my defense I knew

but when he spoke, it was half-heartedly,
as he had done for more than twenty-seven
years in dealing with his wife.

He's really not an invalid you know,
my son replied, but certainly we can
explore some places that might do.

My son the wimp, had uttered
his best thought and all but
signed the papers in his mind.

What's all the fuss about my
wetting sheets? It only happens
twice a week—I don't awake in time.

If I'd been a cat, I would already
have been put to sleep. Has my whole
life then been reduced to this?

She had learned to punish me
in mean and subtle ways,
first for my remaining still alive

when her own father died so young.
She used to wake me softly in the night,
gently change the linen and kindly

touch my face and tell me not to fret.
Now, instead of waking me,
she lets me lie where I have wet

until I get up and put the sheets
into the laundry bin.
She doesn't talk to me, except when
guests are here and then she says
Dad, tell them how old you are, as
though I had broken yet another rule.

No longer does she put out breakfast food,
except on weekends, when my son is home.
She says that I should know where things

are kept, although I really don't, I just forget.
In fairness, I should say I have become a grouch
and know I am not that easy to be with.

I guess it will be Belle that takes me in and
somehow I feel it's a relief
to start the final chapter of my life
among two hundred persons just like me.

The Bread Line

I never thought I'd end up on the bread line.
At Belle, I wait with all the needy folks.
Freebies come our way from time to time.
Keeps our minds off heart attacks and strokes.

I never thought I'd yearn for cherry blintzes.
The kind we used to buy along Broadway
or turn into those penny-pinching grinches,
hoarding all that came in sight each day.

I've never cared at all for pumpernickel,
or multi grain or pita though I try,
German Jewish Rye just makes me sickle
and that goes double for their shepherd pie

I never thought I'd spend my hours lining
up for doughnuts and all the sugar treats.
I never thought I'd spend my mornings pining
to walk as once I had down busy streets.

I'll bet this bread was dry and stale on Monday,
stuff that folks would never want to buy.
The French baguettes are weapons and they still may
be the death of me should someone try.

The Football Game

I died this morning early
with less attention given than I had
hoped. Not an uncommon occurrence
here at Belle. As instructed,
I'd always hang the red knitted flag

on my door knob the night before
and when I wasn't able to retrieve it,
then Mrs. P. would know I had become
quite ill or worse. It was much worse.

But passing was not as bad as I had
feared. There was a dream
that I was running for a football pass
and fell into the river. I gasped for

breath, still holding high the ball and soon
my gasping stopped. And that was it.
Belle's policy was to remove the
players quickly by the fire escape

so as not to inconvenience other guests,
gathered for their breakfast in the foyer.
I smile thinking that Mrs. P. would
lose no time in having my old room

cleaned so it could be given to
another—someone waiting for the coming
football game.

Nine Sonnets and Two Verses from *Charles*

The following sonnets and verses were selected from
Charles written in the late 1950s
upon the untimely death of my brother.

My appreciation for and apology to Racine and Corneille
for my loose and fanciful treatment of rhyme and meter
in my sonnets for Charles.

I

Another came and told me you were dead.
That you had taken flight before the sun
And from this world of mortal pain you've fled
To dwell among the stars till day is done.
Shall I believe this tongue that whips my heart
Like willow branches whipping in the rain?
As for my soul, I fear it will depart
To leave my flesh to ne'er return again.
Shall we no longer stand upon the hill,
Or work the fields from early morn until
Fatigue and darkness take their nightly stand?
Your death I'll doubt till I hear it from you.
Then shall I die, for no more can I do.

II

'Twas long before the ending of the day;
In sun two brothers walked a lively pace.
Each trying now and then to lead the way,
Till they upon a mount came face to face
With Time. "Please let us see tomorrow's hand
That of the future we may both be told."
Said they who were the owners of that land,
And bribed old Time to stop with yellow gold.
Time had a hoary head and hateful glance
For jealous of the young and strong was he.
Then laughingly he took his bag of chance
And peered within to see what there would be.
"To thee I give a death in early years—
Now then to thee a life of pain and tears."

III

Could I be wrong in saying crime was done
When darkness thought the day had spent its time
A chilly breath to blow into the sun
And make to sound at noon the midnight chime?
For so with summer Nature played its game
Causing buds to drop from bush and tree.
To fields in May the snows of winter came
Chilling, killing all that was to be.
Could I be wrong in saying that I fear
Our prayers and wishes He'll no longer heed?
The heaven of our youth will disappear
While silent altars now ignore our need.
If I be wrong, why has a youth grown ill?
Why does he sleep so soon a sleep so still?

IV

Une chemise blanche pour son âme—
Toute tachée de rouge par sa mort.
Du père, le fils ainé portrait la flamme,
Car l'autre était trop jeune et pas si fort.
D'un sang unique, il ne reste que moi
Pour faire ce qu''il faut de notre race
On craint mon frère la force fût en toi.
Je tremble du chagrin qui me menace.
Une chemise blanche pour espoir,
L'espoir s'en va—et tout le monde pleure.
Des son départ, on ne voit que le soir.
Sans le soleil, je ne sais guère l'heure.
Viens me prendre dans l'éternelle nuit—
Et encore une haleine et je te suis.

V

Pourquoi dors-tu un sommeil si tranquille?
La grande étoile est déjà dans sa tour.
Une charrue attend la main servile.
Faut-il que je commence seul le jour?
Cette nuit j'ai eu un rêve affreux.
Tu vas, peut-être rire en l'écoutant.
Mais je me sens quand même malheureux
Car tu m'est cher mon Charles. Et maintenant
Le rêve: On dirait un désert sacré
Et tu y es—tes bras couvert de sable,
Ta poitrine rouge—ton coeur blessé.
Tes yeux regardent au ciel—le ciel coupable.
La lune en haut est sourde à mes discours.
Doucement la nuit arrive—tu dors toujours.

VI

When winter winds turn grey the morning sky
And chase the frightened leaves from hill to dell,
A tear of yesteryear comes to my eye
Remembering how we said our last farewell.
You knew as I did know that youth was spent,
Though young in mind and body still were we.
To drifting time sometime some joy is lent,
But joy in leaving asked a lender's fee.
Oh, much too softly did I kiss your cheek,
Too light was our embrace, too gay the tone.
Too quickly did I leave your side to seek
A place where I might weep aloud alone.
When winter winds turn grey the morning sky,
A tear of yesteryear comes to my eye.

VII

Count breath for breath I shall not live so long
As thou who issue forth the mortal proof,
Still climbing from a paining world of wrong,
While I shout rhymeless verses from this roof
That reach thee not. Which one of us is dead?
From timeless darkness I succeeded thee.
The womb unique gave thee the path ahead,
To spark my step that I no pits should see.
Count word for word I shall not say so much,
Though anguishly I scream from tongue and pen.
What virtue can be found in sound as such,
When silence rules the death of noble men?
In counting then be happy with this lot.
As one can see, I living, start to rot.

VIII

Where flows that dear inflected blood?
In blackest soil a mixture hath thou made,
Thus turning golden sand to crimson mud,
That thirsty trees may throw a longer shade.
For so in life thy destiny was seen
When insects by the hundreds came to drink.
While sucking spreading larva to the spleen
These parasites thy span of life to shrink.
And so, dear one, the mark of time was set,
Each straining paining hour moved slowly by.
The hands of gods or men could naught but let
An end come swiftly—as a hurried sigh.
Let sun and sand then rid thee of this pain—
That thou from arid earth may flow again.

IX

Would he were here to hear the tempest wild
To see the darkened heavens red with heat,
And touch once more the forehead of a child—
Again to be himself in Nature's beat.
Could but one moment of one moment spent
Glow forth tonight as glows that distant star
Within the breast of one whose spark is lent
By nameless shapes that mock him from afar.
But no, the night of thee shall give no trace
Or shall the ended day recall the morn,
All that has been becomes but breath in space,
When human life from living flesh is torn.
Devoted is thy brother's heart to thee,
While still it beats, devoted it will be.

The Wedding

Wine into each cup was poured
and music sounded gay.
Many cheers of laughter rose
to bless their wedding day.
But he who stood the first of guests
trembled as in pain.
For by the window saw he fall
a sort of blackish rain.

To the feasting hall went they,
their faces round with song.
The bride and groom both smiled to hear
that love and life were long.
But he who stood the first of guests
trembled as in pain.
For by the window saw he fall
a sort of blackish rain.

Then thirty wedding guests stood up
to tell the charms of rain.
But he who was the dearest guest
trembled as in pain.
Each voice grew still, each eye was fixed
upon this chosen friend.
So quietly he stood and said,
"Too little can we mend.
I thank the thirty who have tried
to clean the deadly stain.
For thirty months the groom won't hear
or see the blackish rain."

As on that day—the wedding day,
the congregation prayed.
But groom from arms of tearful bride
into the earth was laid.

Dusk

Behold my friend the puffs above,
that hurry to the west,
followed there by half a moon
which seems to pause in rest.

This chestnut tree would stretch its
branches to the graying sky.
A scented breeze comes pressing through
and leaves a gentle sigh.

The golden rays of sunny days
are chilled at last by night.
And shadows circle in a dance
to fill my heart with fright.

A nightingale upon my left
comes to clear the gloom.
Now I'll climb eleven steps
to gain my lighted room.

Although my eyes and mind are weary,
still more clearly must I see,
for they must serve to tell a brother
just what living means to me.

www.ingramcontent.com/pod-product-compliance
Lightning Source LLC
Chambersburg PA
CBHW031139090426
42738CB00008B/1156